ANGEL TO ANGEL

A MOTHER'S GIFT OF LOVE

Walter Dean Myers

HarperCollins*Publishers*

To Viola Law
Big Sister and sometimes —Mother

Photograph "Bright Eyes," below "Angel to Angel," by Hal Gould.
Photograph on second page of "Furniture"
used by permission of the Colorado Historical Society.
The remaining photographs are from the author's collection.

Library of Congress Cataloging-in-Publication Data
Myers, Walter Dean, date
    Angel to angel : a mother's gift of love / Walter Dean Myers.
        p.   cm.
    Summary: An illustrated collection of poems about African American children and
their mothers.
    ISBN 0-06-027721-1. — ISBN 0-06-027722-X (lib. bdg.)
    1. Afro-American children—Juvenile poetry.   2. Afro-American families—
Juvenile poetry.   3. Mother and child—Juvenile poetry.   4. Children's
poetry, American.   [1. Mother and child—Poetry.   2. Afro-Americans—Poetry.
3. American poetry.]   I. Title.
PS3563.Y48A84   1998   97-17498
811'.54—dc21   CIP
                                                                          AC

1 2 3 4 5 6 7 8 9 10
❖
First Edition

Also by Walter Dean Myers

BROWN ANGELS

GLORIOUS ANGELS

NOW IS YOUR TIME!
The African-American Struggle for Freedom

THE RIGHTEOUS REVENGE
OF ARTEMIS BONNER

SCORPIONS

THE STORY OF THE THREE KINGDOMS

I once saw a public television program that showed the reactions of babies to their mothers. A mother's smile would bring an instant, similar response from the child; a mother's frown would be reflected in a worried look on the face of the child. Will anyone ever know how close we are to our mothers? How much the bonding between mother and child affects our lives?

Probably, I've always wanted to do this book. Thumbing through my collection of photographs, I'm always bowled over by pictures of mothers and children. I look for similarities in their expressions, or how comfortable they seem with each other. I know that some of the photos in my collection are over a hundred years old and may not be actual mother and child, but it doesn't matter. An aunt or a grandmother will often take the place of a biological mother. It's the feelings of love that define the relationship.

On a different level, maybe I'm looking for an image I think

would fit my own case. The woman who gave birth to me died when I was not quite two. I don't have an undisputed image of her, and no picture of me with her. I look at these pictures, pictures of children leaning against their mothers, standing in the shadows of their strengths, of their love, and I am made whole.

The hard task was to select the images to use for the book. There were so many layers of beauty from which to choose, so many feelings to put on display, so many moments captured by the camera for which I had to search for words. Ultimately the images spoke to me, reminding me of the precious moments I have spent with the woman who became Mother for me. How careless of her not to have left a picture of us together. Perhaps this book is that picture.

Walter Dean Myers

Angel to Angel

Speak softly in the morning
And light it with your smile
You will soft-speak "Mama"
And I will soft-speak "Child"

Or I will soft-speak "Bluebirds"
And you can soft-speak "Breeze"
And I will spend the summer day
With an angel on my knees

Trees

I am a tree
Strong limbed and deeply rooted
My fruit is bittersweet
I am your mother

You are a tree
A sapling by the river
With buds straining for the winter sun
You are my child
Together we are a forest
Against the wind

Pinehurst, N.C. March 24, 1907.

Sunday

"You can't get good turnip greens," Grandpa said,

"Now that Big Sam has passed away."

"They're good if you can fix them," Grandma said.

"Don't let the texture boil away."

"You can't just leave them like you do collards."

Mama mixed corn bread in a pan.

"I can't stand no mushy greens, mushy rice

Or a preacher without a plan."

"Mushy old greens and a no-plan preacher!

You got to hook them up one day!"

Grandpa laughed and ducked

    under Grandma's look

And we went on living Sunday.

Right for Secrets, Left for Love

Mommy tucks me safe in bed
And then turns off the light
Then I listen for I know
How she will end my night

She will whisper ever soft
Sweet words for tiny ears
Right for secrets, left for love
And hugs to ease my fears

In the morning when I wake
The whispers come again
Right for secrets, left for love
That's how my day begins

Furniture

In this square room there is
    A bed, a crib
    an old dresser whose doors
    do not completely close

In this square room there is
    A feeling light as sun
    on a bird's wing,
    the heady scent of baby oil
    a quilt with magic symbols

In this square room there is
    A kettle hissing
    on the two-burner plate
    a cracked porcelain sink
    a door with two sides

In this square room there is
Metal, wood, cotton,
and love
enough furniture
for a small room

Don't Mess With Grandmama and Me

Way down yonder where the tall grass grows
Lives a seven-foot frog with pointy toes
He jumps and he bumps and he swims in the sea
But he'd better not mess
    with Grandmama and me

Grandmama will turn him inside out
She'll make him squeal
    and she'll make him shout
He'll say Oochy ouch
    and say Oo-wee
And be sorry he messed
    with Grandmama and me

Around the corner in a crooked old house
Lives a red-eyed rat and a nine-tailed mouse
They jump on people and they go Hee-heee
But they'd better not mess
    with Grandmama and me

Grandmama will turn them inside out
She'll make them squeal
    and she'll make them shout
Make them say Oochy ouch
    and say Oo-wee
And be sorry they messed
    with Grandmama and me

Down in the cellar underneath the stairs
There are nineteen monsters and fourteen bears
They grab everything that they can see
But they'd better not mess
     with Grandmama and me

Grandmama will turn them inside out
She'll make them squeal
     and she'll make them shout
Make them say Oochy-ouch
     and say Oo-wee
And be sorry they messed
     with Grandmama and me

Over in the bushes in the middle of the park

There's a creepy leepy thing that lives in the dark

It makes scary noises and it stings like a bee

But it better not mess

    with Grandmama and me

Grandmama will turn it inside out

She'll make it squeal

    and she'll make it shout

Make it say Oochy ouch

    and say Oo-wee

And be sorry it messed

    with Grandmama and me

Sleep, Peaceful Child

Sleep, peaceful child

cu-roo, cu-roo

Sleep, peaceful child

cu-roo

Sleep peaceful child

and smile in your sleep Smile in your sleep for me

Awake, lovely child

Awake, awake

Awake, lovely child

Awake

Awake lovely child

and laugh in the sun Laugh in the sun for me

A Serious Poem About Something

Turpey, turpey, top a lot
Clip a padded dabby
Roll a boll and sloll a poll
And flip a lab a rabby

My Child

There is no math between us
no sharp angles to measure the world
No history to define
    Who we are
      or might become

There is no language, no
Words to stir
the moment

Only a curve
in your smile
that somehow matches mine
a familiar glint of morning light
in your eyes

All this vagueness and the
exact art of sending love
across a small space

GANIERE & LAYTON.   3140 State St., Chicago, Ill.

Mother

Memories of you lie
Like autumn leaves
In the field that is my life
I sense the missing parts
As one senses sound
In an empty stadium

What remains: a browned doily you loved
   a brittle iris pressed into an ancient Bible
Echo your tenderness
Leaves fall and fade
And, as I walk through them,
Taller than you ever thought I'd be,
What is left is the comforting
Rustle of love